Christmas Activities

for KS2 Maths

Irene Yates

Brilliant Publications

Published by Brilliant Publications
Sales and despatch:
BEBC Brilliant Publications
Albion Close, Parkstone, Poole, Dorset, BH12 3LL
Tel: 01202 712910
Fax: 0845 1309300
email: brilliant@bebc.co.uk
website:www.brilliantpublications.co.uk

Editorial and marketing:
Brilliant Publications
Unit 10, Sparrow Hall Farm, Edlesborough, Dunstable, Bedfordshire LU6 2ES

The name Brilliant Publications and the logo are registered trademarks.

Written by Irene Yates
Illustrated by Gaynor Berry
Cover design by Z2 Repro
Cover illustration by Chantal Kees

ISBN 978-1-903853-69-6

First published in 2005, reprinted 2008
10 9 8 7 6 5 4 3 2

Printed in the UK
© Irene Yates 2005

Contents

Contents continued...

Introduction

This book has been designed to take you through the term leading up to Christmas, with the targets of the Key Stage 2 Numeracy Strategy autumn term for Years 3–6 specifically in mind. The book, as a whole, covers a wide spectrum of these targets whilst providing lots of fun activities, all linked to Christmas.

The sheets can be used independently and most ask the children to work in the space provided. Each task, or activity, has educational rigour, making the work suitable for introducing a topic or reinforcing it. The sheets are not designed as time fillers and should not be used as such. They are meant to become an integral part of your numeracy planning for the first term of the year.

The reindeers' speech bubbles at the bottom of the sheets are useful starting points for plenary sessions.

The contents page provides brief descriptions of the numeracy objectives for each sheet. Using these brief descriptions you can run down the contents page to find objectives that you may wish to reinforce with any particular child. You can tick them off to remind yourself of targets you have worked on.

Where sheets have specific answers, these are given on pages 62–64.

This book is one of a series of books aimed at making your life easier around Christmas time. The other books in the series are:

Christmas Activities for KS1 Language and Literacy   ISBN 978-1-903853-66-5

Christmas Activities for KS2 Language and Literacy   ISBN 978-1-903853-67-2

Christmas Activities for KS1 Maths   ISBN 978-1-903853-68-9

Have fun!

Lost numbers

Santa is having a terrible night. The elves stuck numbers on the parcels but some of them have fallen off.

Count on in ones for these parcels. Write each number in.

Count on in fives for these parcels. Write each number in.

Count on in twos for these parcels. Write each number in.

How many numbers were lost altogether? ☐

More lost numbers

Santa has lost some of the numbers off his parcels. Can you help him?

Count **back** in ones for these parcels. Write each number in.

408

Count **back** in fives for these parcels. Write each number in.

110

Count **back** in twos for these parcels. Write each number in.

72

Counting backwards what would be the next number in each set of parcels?

Christmas Activities for KS2 Maths

Santa's muddle

The elves have made such a muddle of counting all the sets of presents that Santa has to do it himself.

Please help him.

Santa has this many parcels in a set	Plus these	How many altogether?
243	3	
5	47	
203	6	
5	127	
621	8	
279	10	
86	4	
599	5	
8	27	
365	5	

What number does Santa get if there are another **100** to add to the first set?

Elf muddles

Help the elves to sort out their muddles:

1. Silly Elf has 3 dolls, 2 cars and 1 football to pack. What is the sum of these toys?

2. Happy Elf should have labelled 14 parcels and he's only labelled 6. What is the difference?

3. Big Elf has stacked 5 big parcels, 5 medium sized parcels and 7 small parcels. What is the total number of parcels?

4. Jumpy Elf should have wrapped 6 less parcels than 18. How many should he have wrapped?

5. Lazy Elf has 15 sacks to pack. Little Elf has 23 sacks to pack. How many more does Little Elf have?

6. Hungry Elf has a pound. He bought a sandwich for 65p. How much change did he get?

7. Greedy Elf wants an extra big sandwich which costs 75p, too, but only has 35p. How much more money does he need to buy one?

Write a sum that is the same as 9 + 4.

Christmas decorations

Sam is making Christmas decorations for the tree by cutting out shapes.

Have a look at his shapes and sort them into groups.
Write the letters beside each shape in the table below.

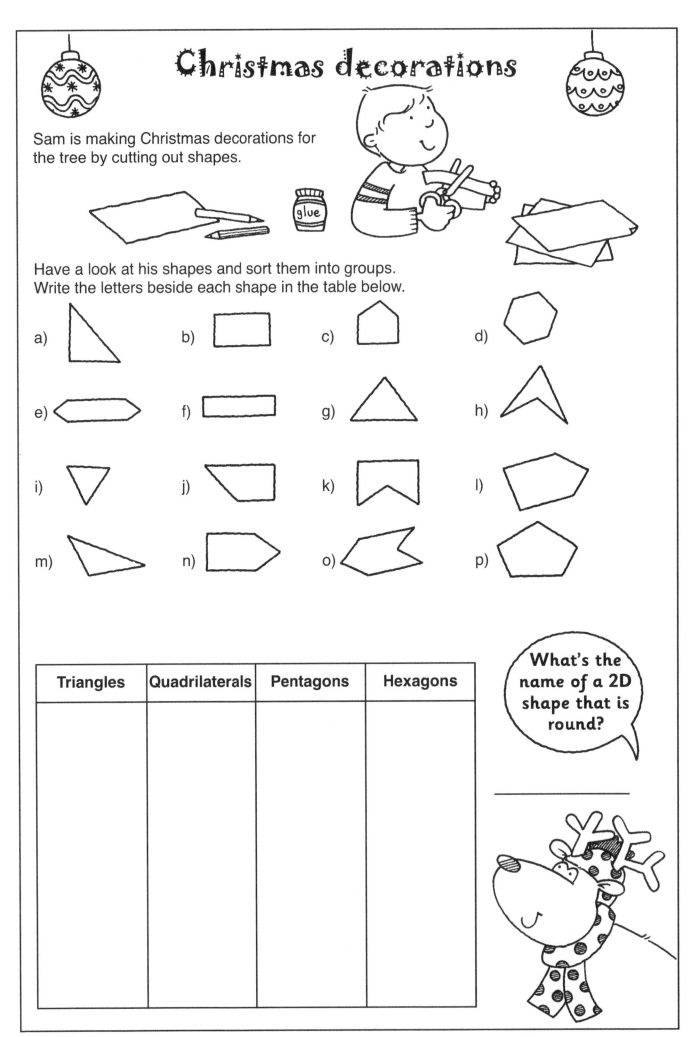

a)

b)

c)

d)

e)

f)

g)

h)

i)

j)

k)

l)

m)

n)

o)

p)

Triangles	Quadrilaterals	Pentagons	Hexagons

What's the name of a 2D shape that is round?

_____

Little Elf's problem

Little Elf is having terrible trouble sorting out his parcel list.
He can't work out the numbers. Santa tells him to stay calm
and work out what the numbers mean, like this:

345	means	300	+	4 tens	+	5 units
	or	300	+	40	+	5

Help him work out these numbers:

134 means

253 means

321 means

472 means

511 means

605 means

791 means

824 means

982 means

Write in words what 1000 means.

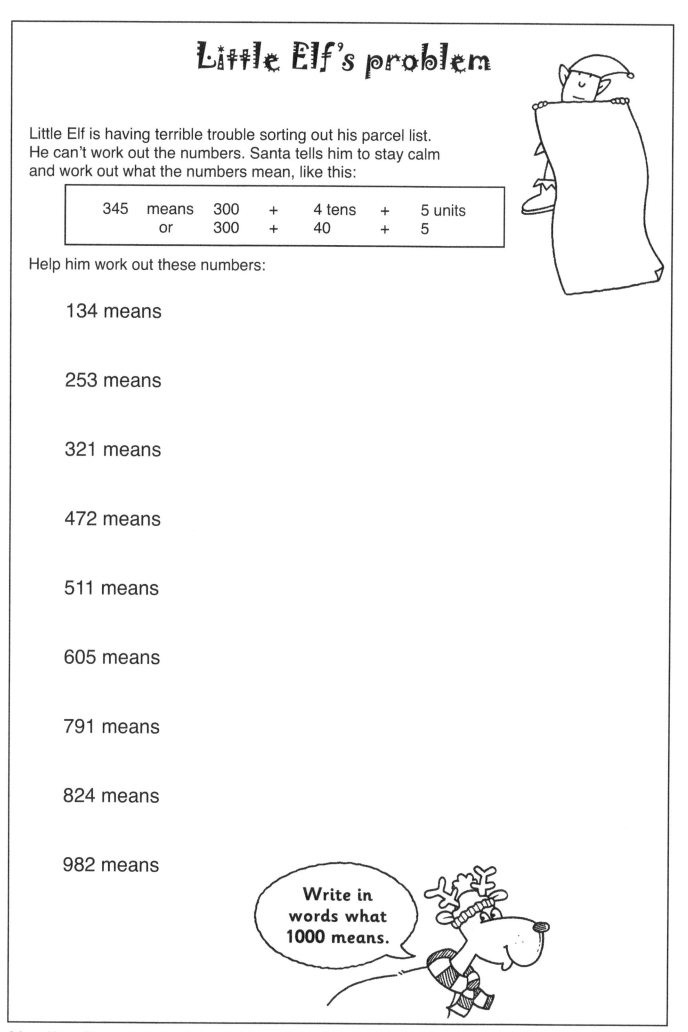

Big Elf's job

Big Elf's job is to sort out all the toys to be wrapped and packed. He has to get the right number each time. Help him by multiplying the way he's done the first one on his list.

3 elves each want 2 dolls

$$3 \times 2 = 6$$

6 elves each want 3 footballs

4 elves each want 4 trains

6 elves each want 1 jigsaw

5 elves each want 3 books

6 elves each want 2 paint sets

8 elves each want 3 Buzz Lightyears

7 elves each want 2 teddies

9 elves each want 2 crayon sets

10 elves each want 5 Power Rangers

7 elves each want 4 Play Stations

I multiply a number by 6 and the answer is 18. What is the number?

Big Elf's puzzle

Big Elf needs to sort out the toys for the other elves. Can you help him write the sums? He's already done the first one.

He has 18 toy cats. How many each can 3 elves have?

$$18 \div 3 = 6$$

He has 10 fluffy rabbits. How many each can 2 elves have?

He has 20 paintboxes. How many each can 5 elves have?

He has 24 books. How many each can 3 elves have:

He has 28 torches. How many each can 4 elves have?

He has 45 squeaky ducks. How many each can 5 elves have?

He has 48 hissing snakes. How many each can 4 elves have?

He has 90 ludo games. How many each can 10 elves have?

He has 27 bouncing frogs. How many each can 3 elves have?

He has 100 trains sets. How many each can 10 elves have?

Turn 18 ÷ 3 = 6 into a multiplication sum:

☐ x ☐ = 18

or ☐ x ☐ = 18

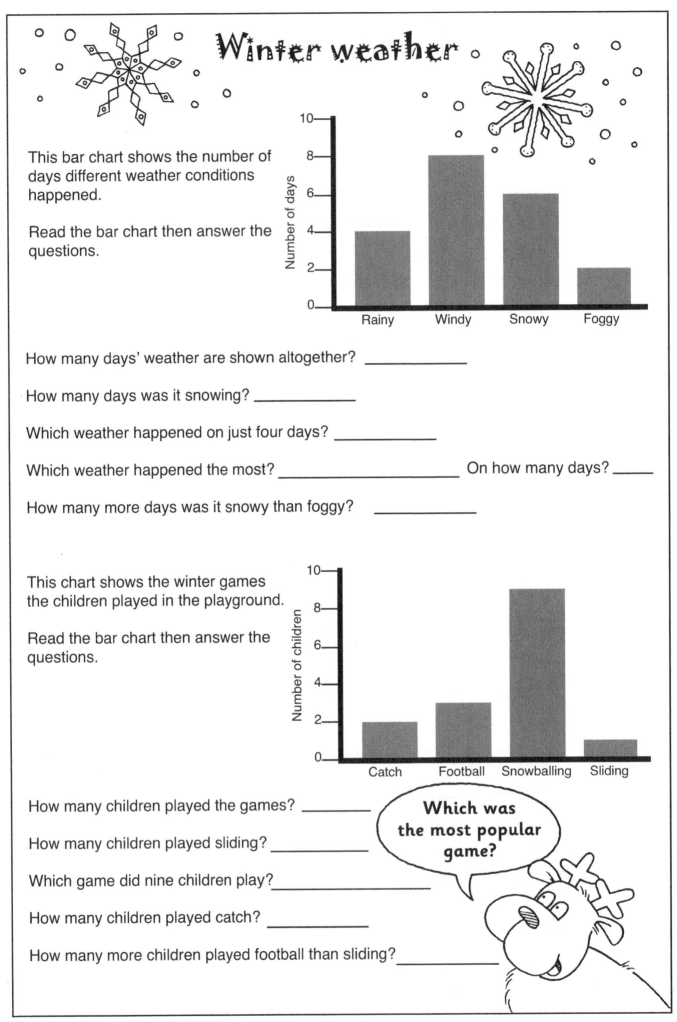

Winter weather

This bar chart shows the number of days different weather conditions happened.

Read the bar chart then answer the questions.

How many days' weather are shown altogether? _____

How many days was it snowing? _____

Which weather happened on just four days? _____

Which weather happened the most? _____ On how many days? _____

How many more days was it snowy than foggy? _____

This chart shows the winter games the children played in the playground.

Read the bar chart then answer the questions.

How many children played the games? _____

How many children played sliding? _____

Which game did nine children play? _____

How many children played catch? _____

How many more children played football than sliding? _____

Which was the most popular game?

Make a Christmas tree bauble

This is how to make a bauble.

You need:

card 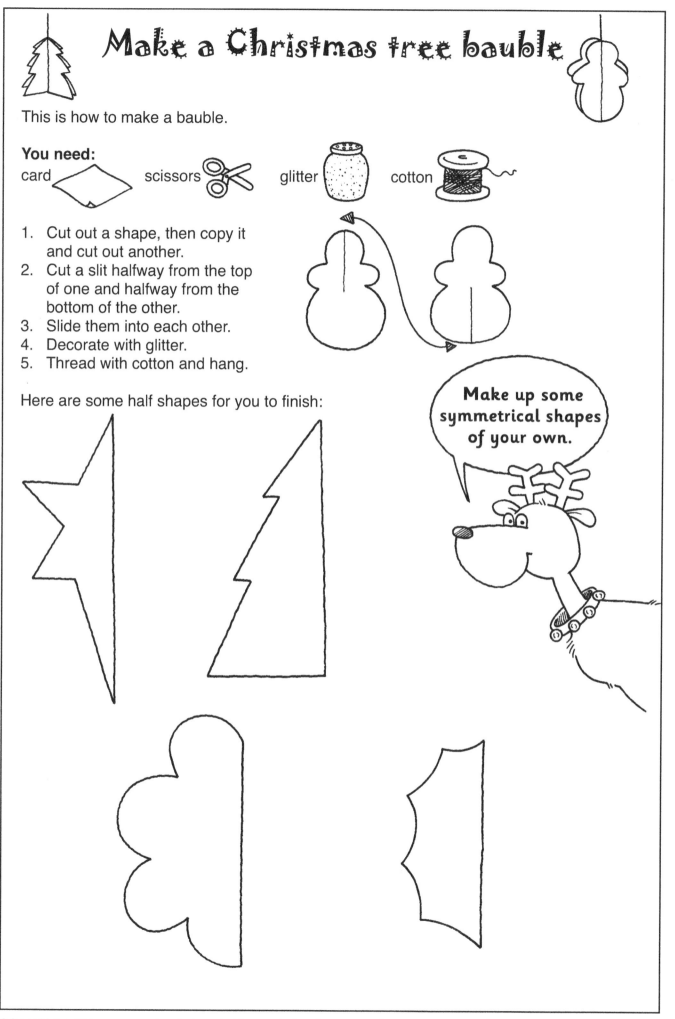   scissors   glitter   cotton

1. Cut out a shape, then copy it and cut out another.
2. Cut a slit halfway from the top of one and halfway from the bottom of the other.
3. Slide them into each other.
4. Decorate with glitter.
5. Thread with cotton and hang.

Here are some half shapes for you to finish:

Make up some symmetrical shapes of your own.

Clever Elf's idea

Clever Elf is showing off how smart he is. He has decided to work in fractions while he's counting out presents. This is the list he gives to Happy Elf. How many should Happy Elf have?

Clever Elf's List		Happy Elf's list
half of 10	=	
a third of 12	=	
a quarter of 20	=	
a tenth of 10	=	
$\frac{1}{2}$ of 8	=	
$\frac{1}{3}$ of 15	=	
$\frac{1}{4}$ of 24	=	
$\frac{1}{10}$ of 50	=	

Colour the fractions of these wholes:

Colour $\frac{1}{4}$ Colour $\frac{1}{3}$ Colour $\frac{3}{4}$ Colour $\frac{1}{2}$ Colour $\frac{1}{10}$

Time's getting on

Santa has only a few hours to deliver all the sacks. He has to keep looking at his watch to see how fast he's going.

Fill in these times for him, using numbers.

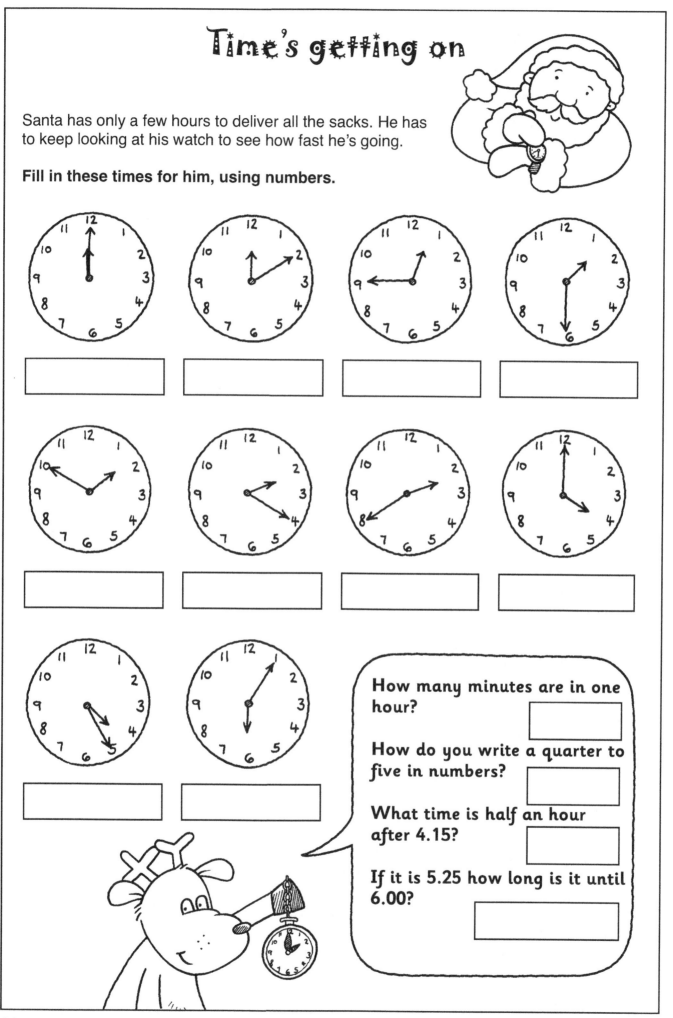

How many minutes are in one hour?

How do you write a quarter to five in numbers?

What time is half an hour after 4.15?

If it is 5.25 how long is it until 6.00?

Elves in trouble

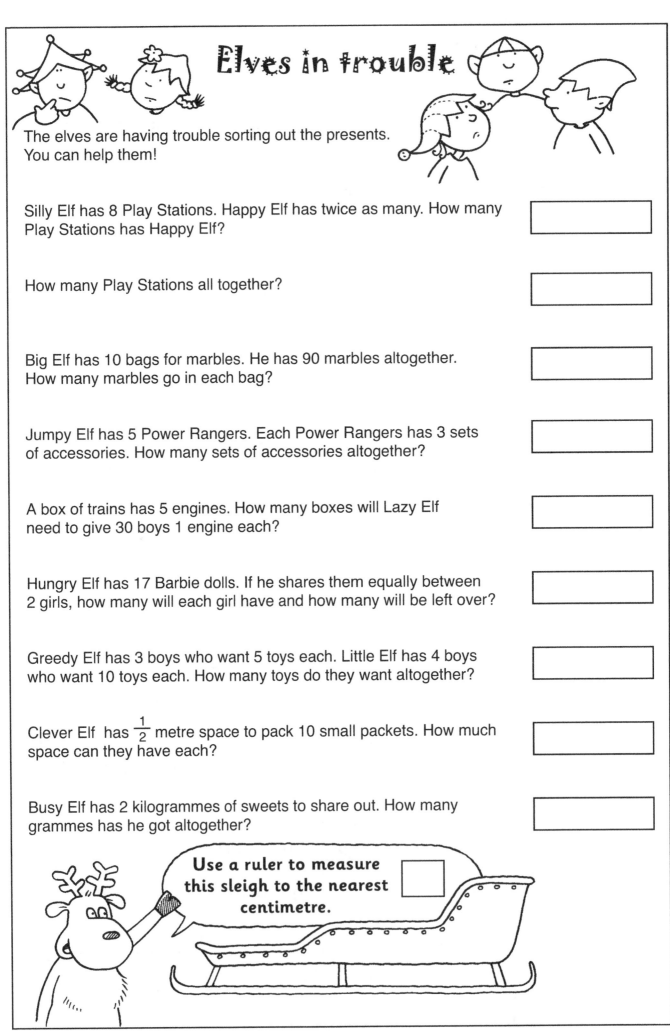

The elves are having trouble sorting out the presents.
You can help them!

Silly Elf has 8 Play Stations. Happy Elf has twice as many. How many
Play Stations has Happy Elf?

How many Play Stations all together?

Big Elf has 10 bags for marbles. He has 90 marbles altogether.
How many marbles go in each bag?

Jumpy Elf has 5 Power Rangers. Each Power Rangers has 3 sets
of accessories. How many sets of accessories altogether?

A box of trains has 5 engines. How many boxes will Lazy Elf
need to give 30 boys 1 engine each?

Hungry Elf has 17 Barbie dolls. If he shares them equally between
2 girls, how many will each girl have and how many will be left over?

Greedy Elf has 3 boys who want 5 toys each. Little Elf has 4 boys
who want 10 toys each. How many toys do they want altogether?

Clever Elf has $\frac{1}{2}$ metre space to pack 10 small packets. How much
space can they have each?

Busy Elf has 2 kilogrammes of sweets to share out. How many
grammes has he got altogether?

**Use a ruler to measure
this sleigh to the nearest
centimetre.**

Mrs Santa does the shopping

Mrs Santa is buying Christmas presents for Santa, the elves and the reindeer. Help her with her money sums.

Reindeer food costs 5p a bag. How many 5p pieces does she need to make 50p?

She has £1.00 to spend equally on 4 elves. How much can she spend on each?

She has three lots of 25p. How much has she got altogether?

She wants to buy 4 new hats at £2.50 each. How much will they cost?

She buys Santa a chocolate star for £1.65. She gives the cashier £2.00. How much change does she get?

After she has spent £2.50, she has 90p left. How much did she start with?

Mrs Santa needs £1.40 to buy a book. She's only got 20p coins. How many does she need?

At the end of the shopping, Mrs Santa has £3.20 left. Santa gives her another £1.80. How much has she got now?

£2.75

Mrs Santa has three 20p pieces, six 5p pieces and two 1 pound coins. Can she buy me this coat?

Christmas Tree Farm

On Christmas Tree Farm, the farmer is keeping a record of all the Christmas trees he sells in one week. Help him fill in the boxes. The first one has been done for you.

Sunday	2156 =	2000	+	100	+	50	+	6
Monday	4863 =	☐	+	800	+	60	+	3
Tuesday	8325 =	8000	+	☐	+	☐	+	5
Wednesday	3982 =	☐	+	900	+	☐	+	☐
Thursday	5829 =	☐	+	☐	+	20	+	☐
Friday	6841 =	☐	+	800	+	☐	+	☐
Saturday	7491 =	☐	+	☐	+	☐	+	☐

Can you answer these questions?

Which day did the farmer sell the most Christmas trees? ☐

Which day did he sell the least Christmas trees? ☐

How many more Christmas trees did he sell on Saturday than Thursday? ☐

Clowns

At the Christmas pantomime, the clowns throw four digits out of a bucket. The digits are:

7   3   8   9

Using the digits, write as many four digit numbers as you can.

Example: 3897

What is the largest four digit number you can make?

What is the smallest four digit number you can make?

Pantomime tickets

Mrs Santa has organised everybody to put on a Christmas pantomime. But somebody has got the tickets muddled up.

Write either < or > for each lot of tickets.

15732		1573
2050		5200
793		1000
1264		1064
6517		6571
25320		25318
999		1999
8085		8058

Put these ticket numbers in order, starting with the smallest first.

1603
630
16003
3601
6803
1638

Christmas tree lights

Jumpy Elf is in charge of putting the lights on all the Christmas trees around Santa's workshop. Each set of lights has a number sequence but the lights won't work if any of the numbers are missing.

Fill in the missing lights.

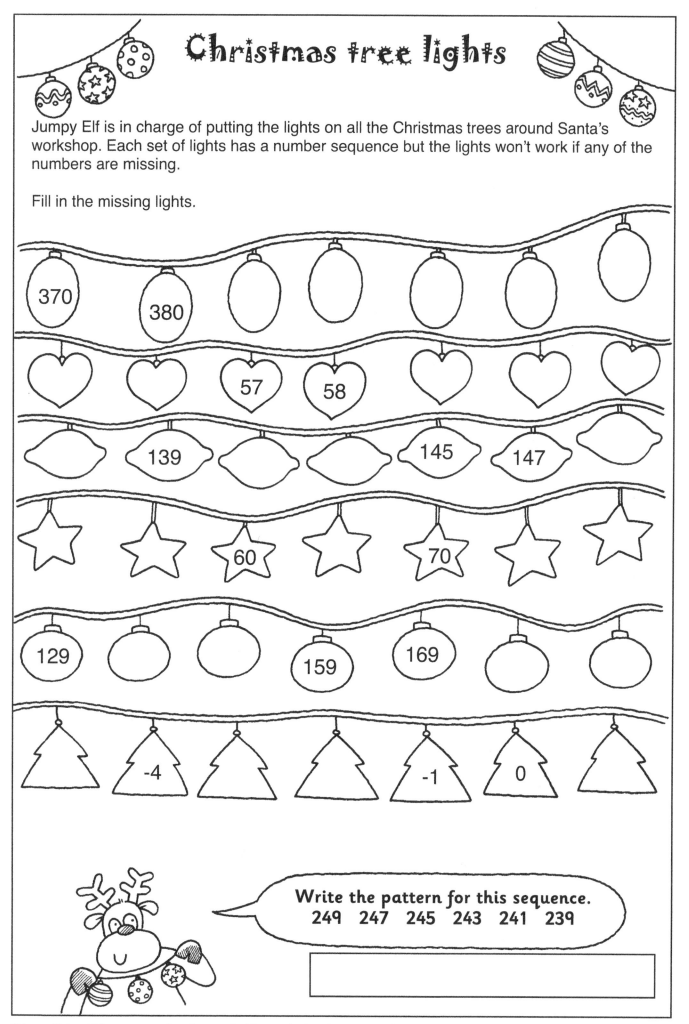

370 380

57 58

139 145 147

60 70

129 159 169

-4 -1 0

Write the pattern for this sequence.
249 247 245 243 241 239

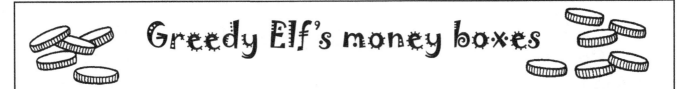

Greedy Elf's money boxes

Greedy Elf has saved hundreds of pennies to spend on Christmas presents. Mrs Santa says she will change them into larger coins if he tells her how much he has got but it's too hard for him to count it all in one go.

Help him to work out how much he has in each of his boxes in pounds and pence.

180p =

295p =

73p =

132p =

605p =

1030p =

220p =

170p =

How much has Greedy Elf got altogether?

How much does he need to make his money up to £40.00?

Christmas shopping

Big Elf has £20.00 to spend and lots of presents to buy. Help him work out what he can buy.

Write your sums at the bottom of the page.

85p

£1.20

colouring

£3.25

£1.20

£1.70

£1.15

45p

35p

55p

£1.30

£1.25

95p

£2.75

80p

£2.05

£2.70

75p

85p

90p   I ♥ You

How much more money does Big Elf need to buy everything?

Sleigh drop

Here is Big Elf's pictogram record of how many sacks have been delivered.

This is his key

⌀ = between 1 and 4 sacks

◯ = 5 sacks

10–11 pm	◯ ◯ ◯ ◯
11–12 pm	◯ ◯ ⌀
12–1 am	◯ ◯ ◯ ◯
1–2 am	◯ ⌀
2–3 am	◯ ◯ ◯ ◯ ◯
3–4 am	◯
4–5 am	

How many sacks were delivered between 2 and 3 am? [ ]

Approximately how many sacks were delivered between 11 and 12 pm? [ ]

28 sacks were delivered between 4 and 5 am. Show it on Big Elf's chart.

When were the least number of sacks delivered? [ ]

Were more sacks delivered before midnight or after midnight? [ ]

Which was the best hour for deliveries? [ ]

At what time were the most sacks delivered? [ ]

Approximately how many sacks were delivered altogether? [ ]

If one sack counted as 10 instead of 5 how many sacks would have been delivered altogether? [ ]

Postman's problems

The postman has so many Christmas cards to deliver!
To make his job easier, he puts the cards in sets of 10.
Help him to count the number of cards and sets.

Number of sets	How many cards? (multiply by 10)
37	
46	
89	
130	
632	
715	

How many sets of 10 altogether? ☐

How many cards altogether? ☐

Number of cards	How many sets of 10 (divide by 10)
130	
250	
970	
1600	
5550	
7190	

How many cards altogether? ☐

How many sets of 10 altogether? ☐

Look at your answers. Write the highest number you find in words.

Look at your answers. Write the lowest number you find in words.

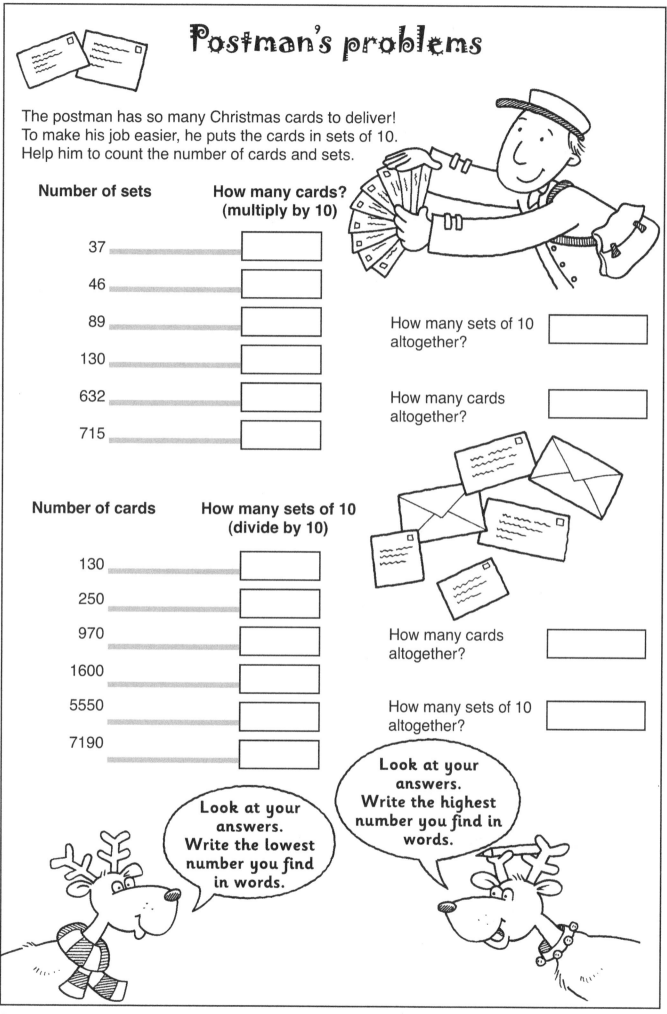

Christmas cakes

This is Mrs Santa's recipe for a Christmas cake:

50g   margarine
40g   brown sugar
60g   flour
1 egg
20g   mixed fruit
20 ml milk

Mrs Santa's recipe will only make enough for 4 people. Write a recipe that would make enough cake for 12 people.

A bag of reindeer food weighs 450g. How much do 5 bags weigh? Write the answer in kg.

Elves' playtime

The elves are having a break. They are playing 'Name the shape' with 3D shapes. These are the six shapes they have found.

Help the elves to put their labels on the correct shapes.

cylinder

cube

cone

pyramid

cuboid

sphere

1. _____

2. _____

3. _____

4. _____

5. _____

6. _____

Can you name these 3D shapes?

A shape with 6 square faces is a _____

A shape with 1 square and four triangular faces is a _____

A shape with 2 square and four rectangular faces is a _____

A shape that is completely curved is a _____

Snowflakes

Did you know that every snowflake is different? They are always symmetrical. They can have several lines of symmetry.

Design six snowflakes, making each design different.
Give each one at least three lines of symmetery.

Make some snowflakes like the ones you have designed, by folding and cutting paper. Open them out and draw all the lines of symmetry.

Chocolate bar

Here is a big bar of chocolate that Santa has had for Christmas.
He's marked it into sections so that he can share it.

Thanks, Santa

$\frac{1}{2}$

$\frac{1}{3}$

$\frac{1}{4}$

$\frac{1}{5}$

$\frac{1}{6}$

$\frac{1}{8}$

$\frac{1}{10}$

Write these fractions in order, starting with the smallest:

$\frac{3}{5}$ $\frac{1}{2}$ $\frac{2}{3}$ $\frac{1}{10}$ $\frac{3}{4}$ $\frac{9}{10}$ $\frac{1}{4}$ $\frac{2}{10}$

If Santa gives $\frac{1}{3}$ to Mrs Santa, how many thirds will he have left?

If Santa eats $\frac{5}{8}$ how many eights will he have left?

Do these:

$\frac{3}{4}$ is the same as $\frac{6}{}$

$\frac{1}{2}$ is the same as $\frac{3}{}$

$\frac{}{6}$ is the same as $\frac{1}{3}$

$\frac{1}{2}$ is the same as $\frac{}{10}$

$\frac{2}{}$ is the same as $\frac{1}{4}$

$\frac{1}{5}$ is the same as $\frac{2}{}$

Grandma goes shopping

At 8.30 am Grandma goes into town to buy lots of presents.
She spends all day at the shops. Put the times on the digital clocks.

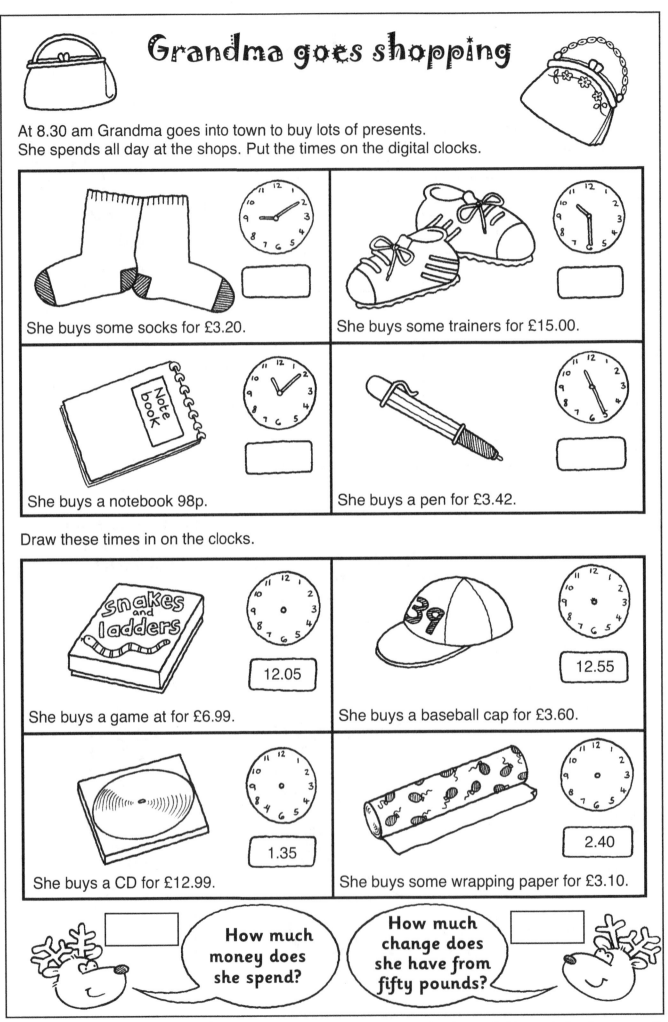

She buys some socks for £3.20.

She buys some trainers for £15.00.

She buys a notebook 98p.

She buys a pen for £3.42.

Draw these times in on the clocks.

12.05

She buys a game at for £6.99.

12.55

She buys a baseball cap for £3.60.

1.35

She buys a CD for £12.99.

2.40

She buys some wrapping paper for £3.10.

How much money does she spend?

How much change does she have from fifty pounds?

Things to think about

1. Little Elf has 90p. How many 7p Christmas cards can he buy?

How much has he left?

2. Lazy Elf has 437 presents to pack. He has done 132. How many has he left to pack?

3. Greedy Elf saves £2.30 a week. He wants to buy a CD that costs £11.50. How many weeks will it take him?

4. Busy Elf has to stick up 5 posters. Each poster needs 4 pins. What fraction of 60 pins will he need?

5. Jumpy Elf has splashed juice on his sheet. Can you put the right digits on his page?

```
    3  2
 +        4
 ─────────
    4  1  3
```

6. Silly Elf can't decide whether to buy a game for £29.00 or a pair of trainers for £45.00. What's the difference in money?

7. Big Elf has been trying to round these numbers up or down to the nearest 10. Help him.

349421   713   556   787

8. Hungry Elf has collected 87 sweets. He has 43 more than Greedy Elf. How many has Greedy Elf got?

9. Happy Elf has divided 72 of his old stickers between 6 elves. How many did they get each?

10. Clever Elf has got three more windows to open on his Advent calendar. What's the date?

Big Elf has some 50g bags of reindeer food. He said I can have four bags. How much food will I get?

Christmas lights

All over the world there are Christmas lights. The elves are having a competition to see who knows the highest numbers.

Help them write these numbers in numerals:

Thirty-five thousand = _____

Five million = _____

Three hundred and eight thousand = _____

Sixty four thousand, four hundred = _____

Three million, four thousand, two hundred = _____

One million, three hundred thousand = _____

Write these numerals in words: | **Hint:** Put the commas in first, to help you |

50000 = _____

5000000 = _____

5000 = _____

5050050 = _____

505050 = _____

500500 = _____

Fill in these boxes:

millions						units

Counting the stacks

Things are hotting up at the grotto. There are so many sacks being sorted that they keep getting counted incorrectly. The elves decide to store them in sets.

Little Elf stores his sacks in sets of five – but can he remember the multiples?

Help him.

10 multiples of 5 ☐☐☐☐☐☐☐☐☐☐

Jumpy Elf decides to store in sets of seven. Help him.

10 multiples of 7 ☐☐☐☐☐☐☐☐☐☐

Happy Elf goes for sets of 9. Help him.

10 multiples of 9 ☐☐☐☐☐☐☐☐☐☐

Clever Elf goes for sets of 12. Help him.

10 multiples of 12 ☐☐☐☐☐☐☐☐☐☐

I'm thinking of a number that is less than 50 and is a multiple of both 5 and 8. What is it? ☐

Hint
Multiples are the answers to multiplication tables.

Which multiple of 9 is between 60 and 70? ☐

So many sacks

There are so many sacks at the grotto that everyone is falling over them. They have to be stored in sets. Help the elves to work out how many there could be in each set.

Jumpy Elf has 48 sacks – but can he remember the factors of 48? Help him.

☐ ☐ ☐ ☐ ☐ ☐ ☐ ☐ ☐ ☐

Lazy Elf has 64 sacks. His factors are:

☐ ☐ ☐ ☐ ☐ ☐ ☐

Greedy Elf has 45 sacks. His factors are:

☐ ☐ ☐ ☐ ☐ ☐

Silly Elf has 81 sacks. His factors are:

☐ ☐ ☐ ☐ ☐

Hungry Elf has 36 sacks. His factors are:

☐ ☐ ☐ ☐ ☐ ☐ ☐ ☐ ☐

Little Elf has 25 sacks. His factors are:

☐ ☐ ☐

Big Elf has a problem. He has 37 sacks. What is his problem?

Weighing the presents

There are lots of presents wrapped up and ready to go. Everything has to be weighed to make sure the sleigh isn't too heavy to fly. It can carry 50kg at a time.

How many grams are in 1kg?

Hint
1 kilogram	=	1000 grams
1kg	=	1000g

How many 50g in 1kg?

How many 200g in 1kg?

How many 500g in 1kg?

How many 2kg in 50kg?

How many 500g in 20kg?

How many 5g make up 200g?

How many 20g make up 20kg?

How many 400g make up 2kg?

How many 500g parcels can go on the sleigh?

Lazy Elf has 51.75kg of parcels. How much has he got to take off to make the sleigh safe?

Mrs Santa's teatime surprise

Mrs Santa has made four huge chocolate cakes for tea. She's decided to cut them into equivalent fractions. The elves have to guess the fraction to get a piece. Help them.

$$\frac{2}{4} = \underline{\quad}$$ $$\frac{12}{16} = \underline{\quad}$$ $$\frac{4}{8} = \underline{\quad}$$ $$\frac{4}{6} = \underline{\quad}$$

$$\frac{5}{10} = \underline{\quad}$$ $$\frac{6}{8} = \underline{\quad}$$ $$\frac{8}{12} = \underline{\quad}$$ $$\frac{15}{20} = \underline{\quad}$$

$$\frac{6}{9} = \underline{\quad}$$ $$\frac{9}{12} = \underline{\quad}$$ $$\frac{7}{14} = \underline{\quad}$$ $$\frac{10}{15} = \underline{\quad}$$

What must you add to $\frac{9}{12}$ to make one whole?

Chocolate cake, anyone?

Mrs Santa's chocolate cakes are going down so well, she decides to make the elves solve fractions before they can have a piece.

First she asks the elves to decide on <, > and =.

Try these:

$\frac{1}{3}$ ☐ $\frac{2}{6}$ $\frac{3}{4}$ ☐ $\frac{2}{3}$ $\frac{4}{3}$ ☐ $\frac{1}{4}$

$\frac{3}{4}$ ☐ $\frac{9}{10}$ $1\frac{5}{8}$ ☐ $\frac{13}{8}$ $\frac{6}{8}$ ☐ $\frac{3}{4}$

Then she asks them to make improper fractions into mixed numbers.

Hint
A mixed number has a whole number and a fraction.

$\frac{7}{5}$ = ☐ $\frac{27}{10}$ = ☐

$\frac{9}{4}$ = ☐ $\frac{12}{3}$ = ☐

Change these mixed numbers into improper fractions.

If you have $\frac{4}{3}$ of chocolate cake, how much do you have? ☐

$2\frac{3}{4}$ = ☐ $1\frac{5}{8}$ = ☐

$1\frac{2}{3}$ = ☐ $1\frac{3}{4}$ = ☐

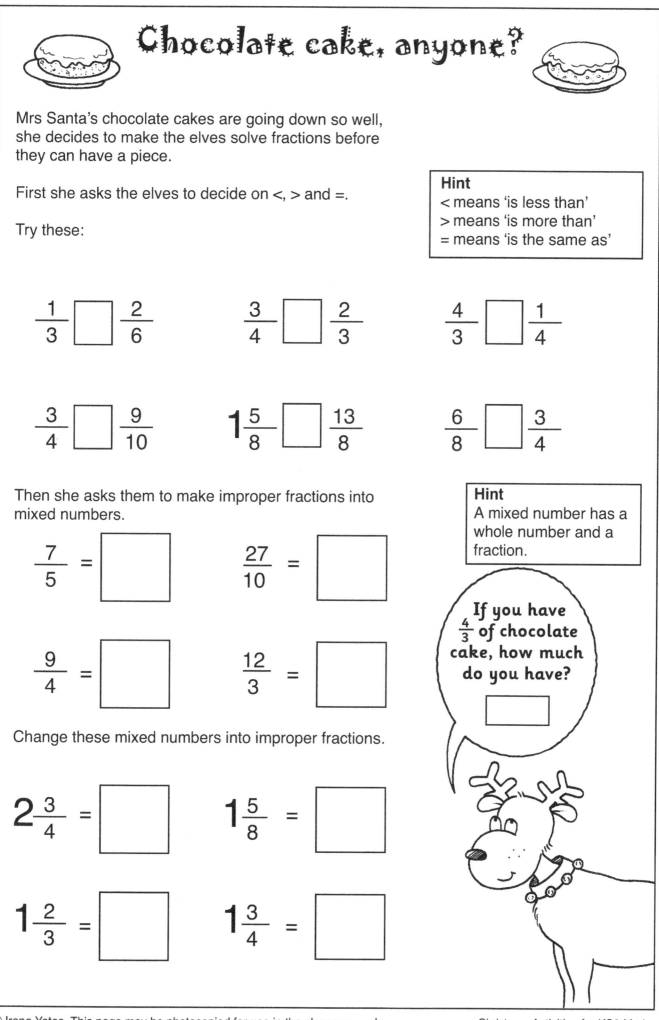

Christmas cards

Santa is hanging up Christmas cards in the grotto.

Every fourth card has fallen down. Draw them in. How many missing cards are there?

1. 2 out of every 5 cards have a robin on them. How many in each 5 do not?

2. Out of 10 Christmas cards, 2 say 'Merry Christmas' and the rest say something else. How many?

3. For every 2 cards with a Christmas tree on, there are 3 with a nativity. How many are there with a nativity?

4. 2 in every 4 cards say 'Love from'. The rest say 'Greetings from'. If there are 8 cards, how many are there of each?

If 3 in every 6 cards come by post and there are 24 cards altogether, how many come by hand?

Christmas dinner

Help busy Mrs. Santa to get the Christmas dinner prepared.

The turkey must be cooked for 20 minutes for each 500g. It weighs 3.25kg. How long must it cook for?

Mrs Santa adds $\frac{1}{2}$ a tablespoon of granules for each litre of stock. What quantity of granules does she use for $2\frac{1}{2}$ litres of gravy?

For the pudding, 50g of sultanas are used for each 25g of raisins. How many sultanas are used for 75g of raisins?

For each big cake she makes, she bakes eight muffins. How many big cakes does she make if she cooks 32 muffins?

Each trifle takes $\frac{1}{2}$ teaspoon of hundreds and thousands. If Mrs Santa uses $3\frac{1}{2}$ teaspoons of hundreds and thousands, how many trifles has she made?

Six elves eat a quarter of the roast potatoes, which is 2 each. How many roast potatoes are there altogether?

Christmas trees at the farm

The Christmas tree farmer decides to make a graph of how many he's sold.
Each mark on the vertical axis stands for 10 trees.

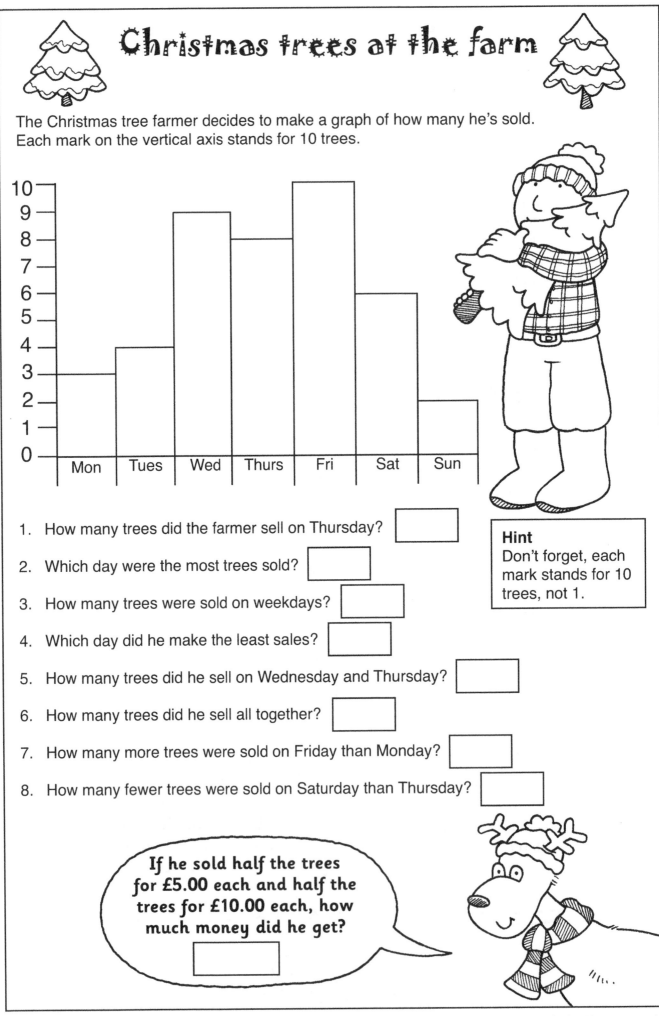

Hint
Don't forget, each mark stands for 10 trees, not 1.

1. How many trees did the farmer sell on Thursday?

2. Which day were the most trees sold?

3. How many trees were sold on weekdays?

4. Which day did he make the least sales?

5. How many trees did he sell on Wednesday and Thursday?

6. How many trees did he sell all together?

7. How many more trees were sold on Friday than Monday?

8. How many fewer trees were sold on Saturday than Thursday?

If he sold half the trees for £5.00 each and half the trees for £10.00 each, how much money did he get?

Christmas tree orders

The Christmas tree farmer has a full order book for the next two weeks.
This is what it looks like.

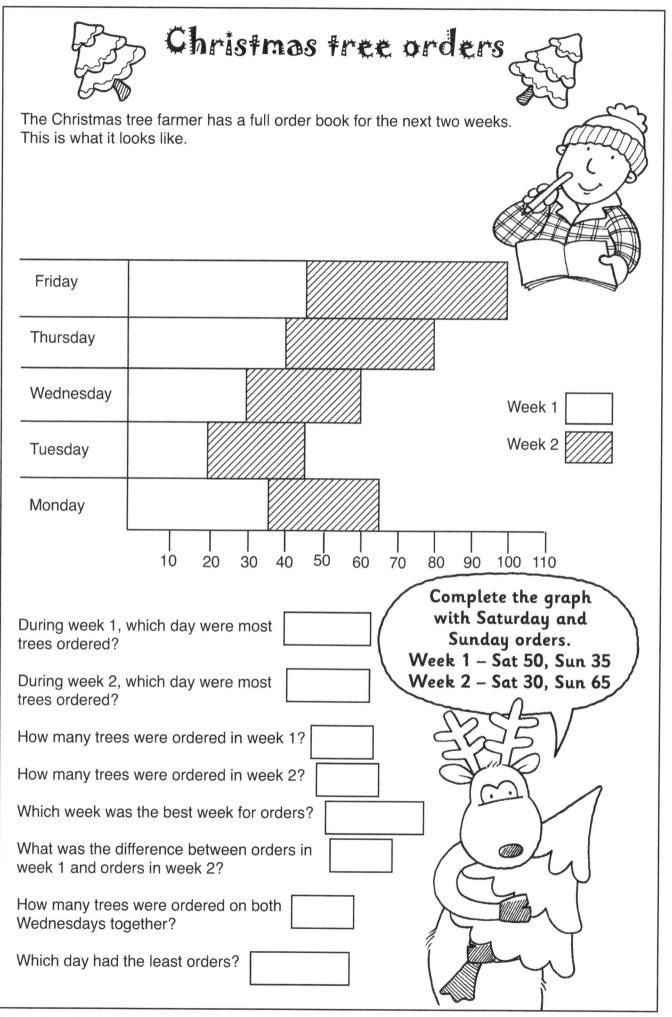

Week 1	☐
Week 2	▨

During week 1, which day were most trees ordered? ☐

During week 2, which day were most trees ordered? ☐

How many trees were ordered in week 1? ☐

How many trees were ordered in week 2? ☐

Which week was the best week for orders? ☐

What was the difference between orders in week 1 and orders in week 2? ☐

How many trees were ordered on both Wednesdays together? ☐

Which day had the least orders? ☐

Complete the graph with Saturday and Sunday orders.
Week 1 – Sat 50, Sun 35
Week 2 – Sat 30, Sun 65

Christmas spending

Little Elf is worried that he's spending too much money.
This is what he's bought in one week.

4 bars of chocolate @ 63p each =

1 book @ £6.99 and a comic @ £2.99 =

1 game @ £12.99, reduced by £5.40 =

A train ticket @ £3.50 + bus fare 90p =

17 Christmas cards @ 35p each =

A disc bag. He didn't know how much it was
but he had £2.25 change from £5.00 =

A pack of pencils @ 19p. He decided to buy
some more so he spent £2.09. How many
more packs did he get? =

5 stamps @ 26p =

**What was the total
amount Little Elf spent?
(Watch out for the
pencil question!)**

**If he only
had £27.08 how much
did he have to borrow
from his mum?**

Christmas crackers!

Time yourself to see how long it takes you to solve these crackers!

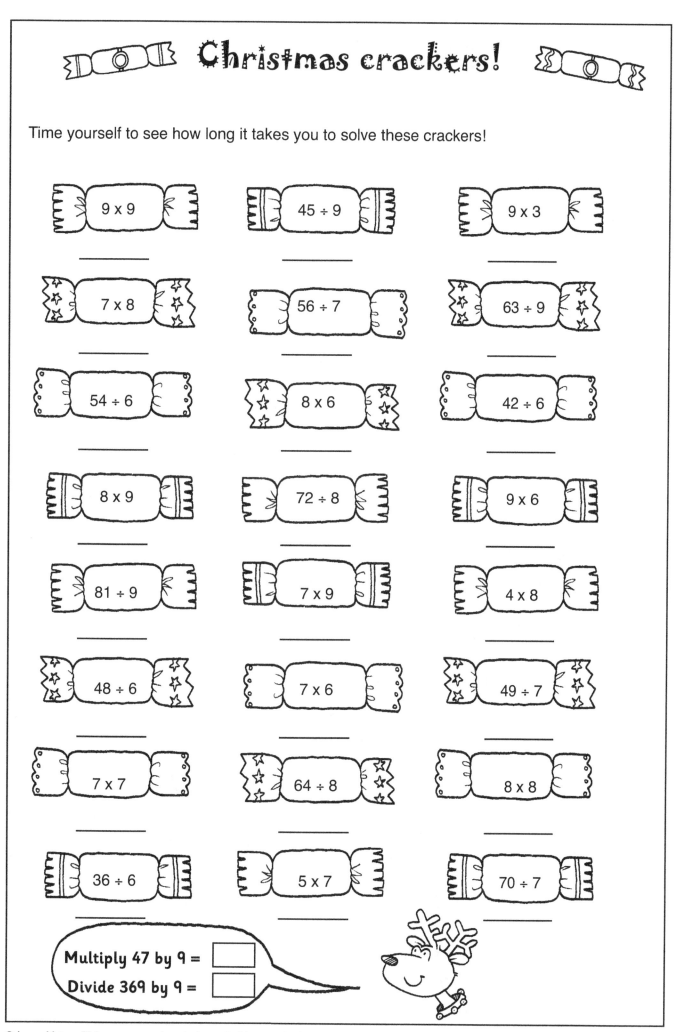

9 x 9 _____

45 ÷ 9 _____

9 x 3 _____

7 x 8 _____

56 ÷ 7 _____

63 ÷ 9 _____

54 ÷ 6 _____

8 x 6 _____

42 ÷ 6 _____

8 x 9 _____

72 ÷ 8 _____

9 x 6 _____

81 ÷ 9 _____

7 x 9 _____

4 x 8 _____

48 ÷ 6 _____

7 x 6 _____

49 ÷ 7 _____

7 x 7 _____

64 ÷ 8 _____

8 x 8 _____

36 ÷ 6 _____

5 x 7 _____

70 ÷ 7 _____

Multiply 47 by 9 = ☐

Divide 369 by 9 = ☐

Christmas stars

Join the stars that are the same:

$\frac{1}{4}$

875%

$\frac{1}{2}$

$1\frac{1}{2}$

150%

430%

1.9

10

50%

0.5

7.75

$4\frac{3}{10}$

1.5

$8\frac{3}{4}$

775%

.25

4.3

190%

$7\frac{3}{4}$

$\frac{100}{10}$

25%

Which is the biggest: 2.6 or $2\frac{4}{5}$? Why?

8.75

$1\frac{9}{10}$

1000%

Christmas wrapping paper

Design some wrapping paper decoration, using symmetrical shapes. Here are some shapes to start you off. Draw in their reflections.

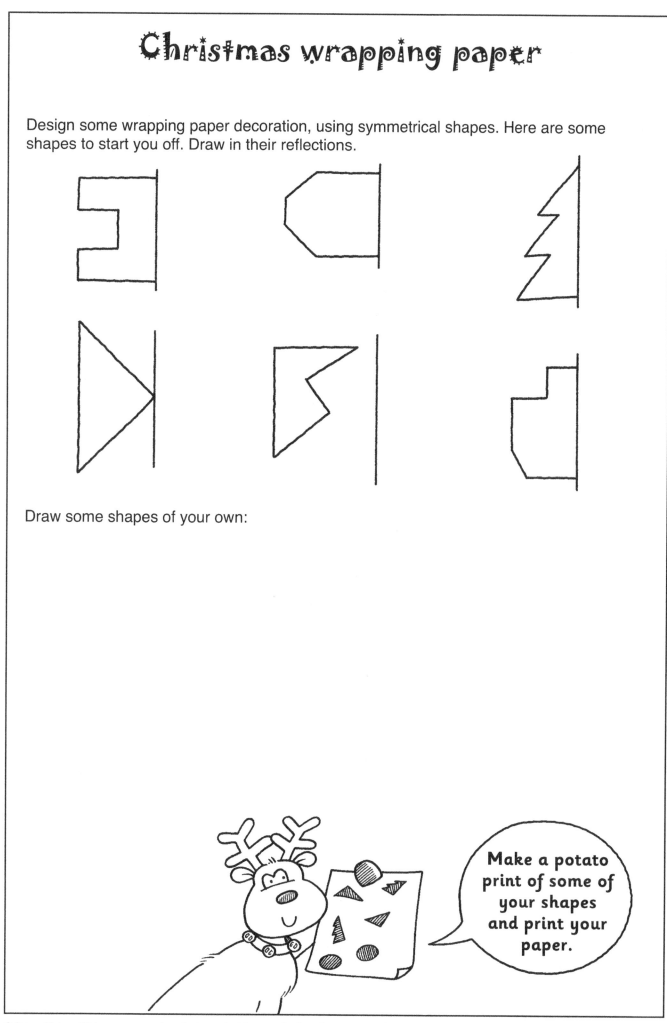

Draw some shapes of your own:

Make a potato print of some of your shapes and print your paper.

Snowballs

The three corner snowballs should total the middle number. Write the missing number:

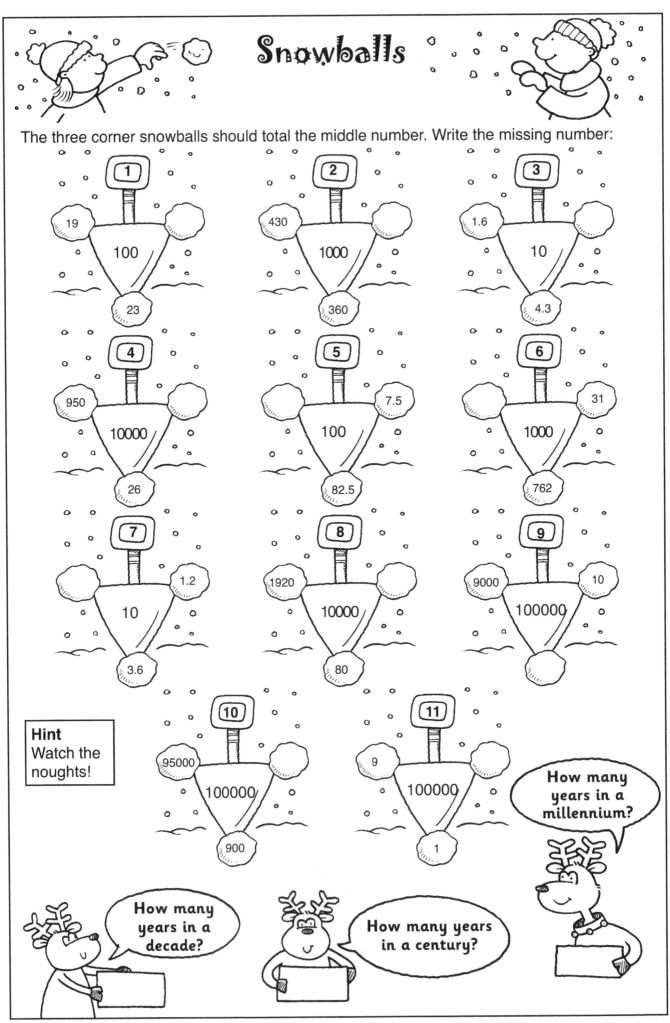

Hint
Watch the noughts!

Santa's night

Write the times he arrives at the different houses, using the 24 hour clock:

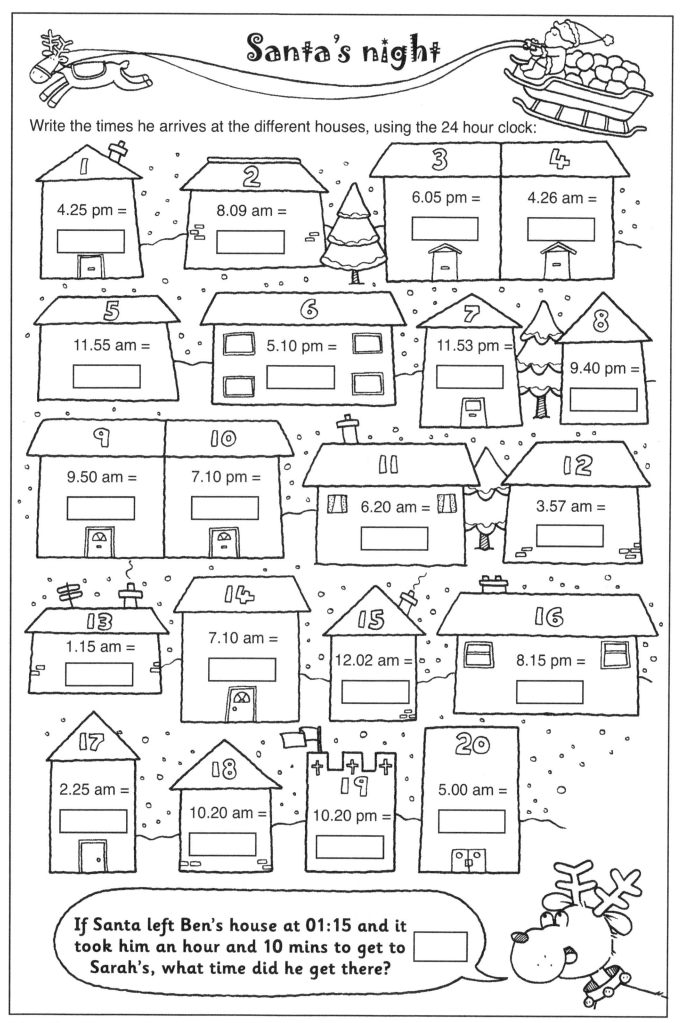

1 4.25 pm =

2 8.09 am =

3 6.05 pm =

4 4.26 am =

5 11.55 am =

6 5.10 pm =

7 11.53 pm =

8 9.40 pm =

9 9.50 am =

10 7.10 pm =

11 6.20 am =

12 3.57 am =

13 1.15 am =

14 7.10 am =

15 12.02 am =

16 8.15 pm =

17 2.25 am =

18 10.20 am =

19 10.20 pm =

20 5.00 am =

If Santa left Ben's house at 01:15 and it took him an hour and 10 mins to get to Sarah's, what time did he get there?

Christmas tree baubles

A number squared is a number multiplied by itself. Fill the answers in on the baubles.

$2^2 =$

$5^2 =$

$3^2 =$

$9^2 =$

$8^2 =$

$12^2 =$

$1^2 =$

$4^2 =$

$7^2 =$

$= 25$

$10^2 =$

$= 81$

$6^2 =$

$= 36$

$11^2 =$

$= 64$

$= 9$

$= 100$

If you have a square piece of wrapping paper that measures 12 cm x 12 cm, what is the area?

Christmas presents

Follow the instructions in the presents below:

Multiply the numbers on the labels of these presents by 100.
Put the answers on the presents.

635   298   111.8   6505   9.35   21.7

Divide the numbers on these presents by 100.
Put the answers on the labels.

23600   46000   5600   1094   26100   5318

Multiply the numbers on the labels of these presents by 1000.
Put the answers on the presents.

62   698   9.05   0.003   413   2731

Write in the missing numbers:

Divide the numbers on these presents by 1000.
Put the answers on the labels.

492000   341800   74   31500   1533000   50

x 100 = 4391

÷ 100 = 0.04

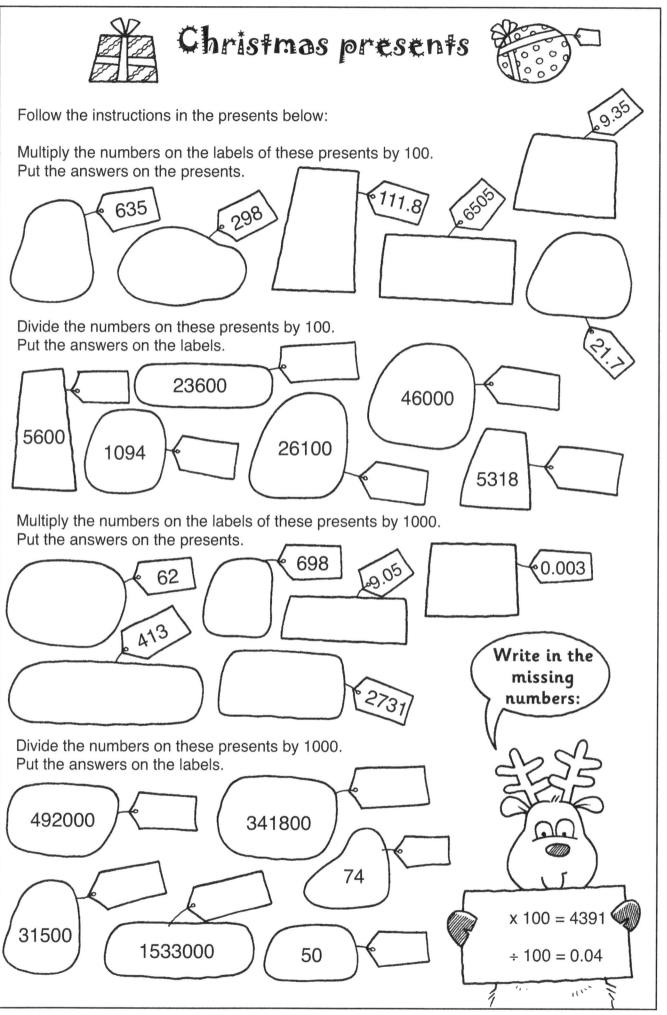

Mrs Santa's puzzles

Mrs Santa has made up some puzzles for the elves.
Help them to solve them.

Write in the missing numbers:

x			
	21	42	56
	15		40
	27	54	72

x	4	8	7
6			42
9			
			40

x	5		6
			48
	35		
9		27	

x			

Make up a puzzle of your own in the blank square.

Reindeer roundabout

1. Big Elf is making a new sleigh. He has a piece of wood 24.48 metres long. He cuts five equal pieces from it. There is a piece 2.48 metres left. How long is each piece of wood?

2. Santa buys these items for the chief reindeer:
★ Antler Shine   £2.60
★ Hoof Clean   £3.97
★ Nose Sparkle   £8.32
★ Reins   £24.98
★ Nosebag   £6.82

How much does he spend?

How much change does he have from £50.00?

3. The first reindeer goes 18.5 kilometres on one journey. He does the journey three times a day on Monday to Friday and four times on Saturday and Sunday. How far does he travel altogether?

4. The reindeer's water bucket holds 3.5 litres. Mrs Santa fills it up from a jug holding 0.5 litres. How many jugs does it take to fill it?

5. The first reindeer takes 37 sacks. The second reindeer takes 52 sacks. How many more does the second reindeer take than the first?

6. Nine bags of reindeer food cost £14.04. How much does one bag cost?

reindeer food

How much Nose Sparkle could I get for £41.60?

Christmas teatime

For tea, there are mince pies and mini yule logs. There are 12 items altogether. The ratio of mince piece to mini yule logs is 1:3.
Draw them on the plates.

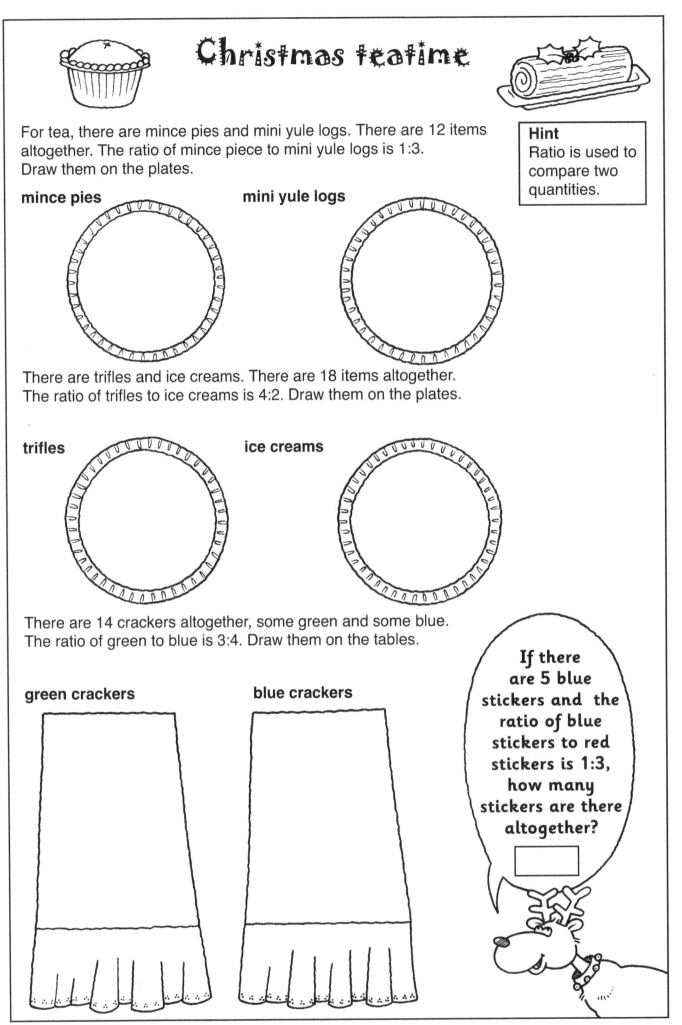

mince pies

mini yule logs

There are trifles and ice creams. There are 18 items altogether.
The ratio of trifles to ice creams is 4:2. Draw them on the plates.

trifles

ice creams

There are 14 crackers altogether, some green and some blue.
The ratio of green to blue is 3:4. Draw them on the tables.

green crackers

blue crackers

If there are 5 blue stickers and the ratio of blue stickers to red stickers is 1:3, how many stickers are there altogether?

Lunchtime!

Mrs Santa is putting out the Christmas Eve lunch.

1.   She gives each of the 12 elves two sausages on sticks each, from 24. What proportion of the whole does each elf have?

2.   3 elves share 6 pitta breads equally between them. How many does each elf have? What is the proportion of the whole?

3.   Little Elf doesn't like pizza fingers. He gives his share to Greedy Elf, who now has 2 shares from a pizza that was divided into 5. What proportion of the whole does greedy Elf have?

4.   There are 100 chocolate biscuits. Mrs Santa shares them out amongst 10 elves. What proportion does each elf get?

5.   There are 6 apples and 24 oranges. What proportion of all the fruit is apples?

6.   There are 36 fizzy drinks poured out. If there are 9 left at the end of lunch, what proportion of drinks were drunk?

Hint
The proportion is the fraction of the whole.

The twelve elves split up after lunch. Four go shopping, five go to play football. What proportion of the whole do neither?

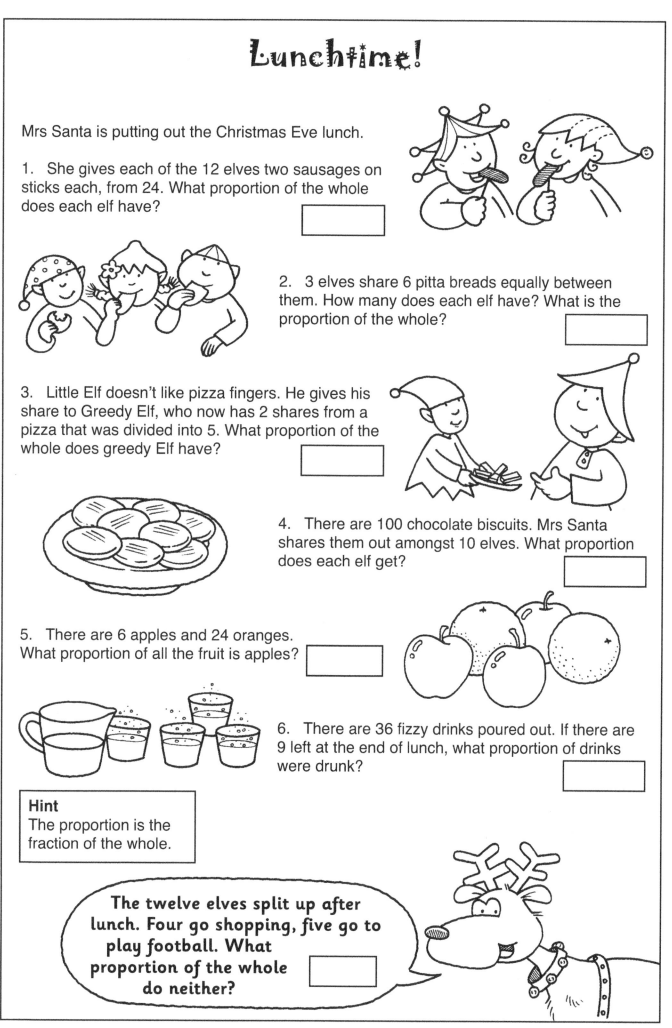

 # Starry, starry night

Its midnight on Christmas Eve and the black sky is full of stars. The elves are trying to count them but they keep going wrong. Help them.

1   3584 add 800 =

2   1642 subtract 80 =

3   Increase 290 by 97 =

4   38 + [ ] = 100

5   83 + [ ] = 200

6   [ ] + 51 = 100

7   250 + [ ] = 1000

8   453 + [ ] = 1000

9   [ ] + 239 = 1000

10   1000 + [ ] = 1000

11   Decrease 98 by 63 =

12   Total 753 and 99 =

13   Take 89 from 913 =

14   100 − [ ] = 35

15   200 − [ ] = 13

16   300 − [ ] = 162

17   1000 − [ ] = 175

18   1000 − [ ] = 340

19   1000 − [ ] = 701

20   10000 − [ ] = 99

Make the points of the stars add up to 1000.

33

92

306

461

[ ]

Packages

The Christmas packages come in all sorts of interesting shapes.
Clever Elf has drawn some of the 2-D shapes he's noticed.
Can you name the shapes he's drawn?

How is a square different to a rhombus?

Hint
The shapes are trapezium, rhombus, kite, rectangle, parallelogram and square. But which is which?

Santa's instructions

Put half of the dolls over there. Put four sixths of the cars over there. Put twelve twentieths of the Playstations over there!

Big Elf can't sort out Santa's fractions. Help him simplify them.

Do it like this:

$$\frac{6}{12} = \frac{6}{12} \div \frac{3}{3} = \frac{2}{4} \div \frac{2}{2} = \frac{1}{2}$$

$$\frac{9}{15} =$$

$$\frac{9}{21} =$$

$$\frac{5}{15} =$$

$$\frac{12}{20} =$$

$$\frac{8}{32} =$$

$$\frac{6}{24} =$$

$$\frac{12}{15} =$$

$$\frac{12}{20} =$$

$$\frac{8}{12} =$$

Make these fractions as complicated as you can!

$$\frac{1}{2} \quad \frac{2}{5} \quad \frac{2}{3} \quad \frac{3}{4}$$

Final count

Each Boxing Day, the elves and Santa do a final count of all the toys delivered that Christmas. It gets quite difficult so they usually round up or down to the nearest 10, 100 or 1000. Help them.

Round these numbers:

		To the nearest 10	To the nearest 100	To the nearest 1000
Dolls	153289			
Trains	987515			
Skipping ropes	612004			
Drums	794688			
Computers	1458454			
Gameboys	92645			
CDs	415473			
Personal stereos	655464			

Hint
Numbers that are half-way or over are rounded up. Below halfway they're rounded down.

Write 23467132 in words, rounded to the nearest thousand.

Countdown to big day

Little Elf is the one who has to keep a check on the time.
Help him.

1. The sleigh leaves for a test run at 7.30 am and gets back at 10.45 am. How long did it take?

2. Lazy Elf starts packing a sack at 7.00 pm and finishes at 8.10 pm. How long did it take him?

3. Mrs Santa is planning the Christmas lunch. It will take 3 hours, 50 minutes to cook. It needs to be ready by 1.30 pm. What time should she start?

4. Santa needs to get himself dressed up and check all the sacks. It takes him 1 hour 10 minutes to get ready and 2 hours 20 minutes to check the sacks. If he starts at midday, what time will he be ready?

5. One of the sleighs breaks down. It's taken to be fixed at 8.30 am and collected at 2.15 pm but it's actually been ready for 45 minutes. How long did the actual repair take?

6. Santa needs to be at the North Pole by 2.30 am. If it takes 1 hour 30 minutes to get to the reindeer ready and the journey takes 55 minutes, what time does he need to start?

If the reindeer take 35 minutes to eat their breakfast and 10 minutes to have a drink of water, then 25 minutes to be reined together, how long does it take to get them ready?

Christmas compass

Clever Elf is in charge of navigating.

Fill in all his compass points.

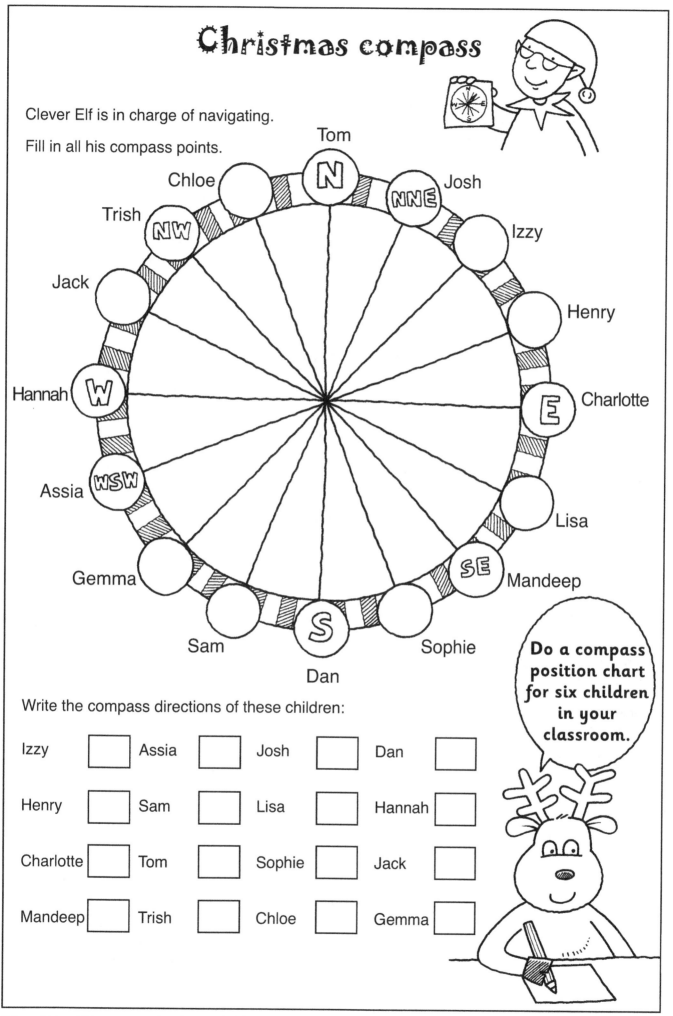

Write the compass directions of these children:

Izzy		Assia		Josh		Dan	
Henry		Sam		Lisa		Hannah	
Charlotte		Tom		Sophie		Jack	
Mandeep		Trish		Chloe		Gemma	

Do a compass position chart for six children in your classroom.

Answers

Page 6
362, 363, 364, 365, 366, 367, 368, 369, 370; 30, 35, 40, 45, 50, 55, 60, 65, 70; 34, 36, 38, 40, 42, 44, 46, 48, 50
Reindeer: 27

Page 7
407, 406, 405, 404, 403, 402, 401, 400, 399; 105, 100, 95, 90, 85, 80, 75, 70, 65; 70, 68, 66, 64, 62, 60, 58, 56, 54
Reindeer: 398, 60, 52

Page 8
246, 52, 209, 132, 629, 289, 90, 604, 35, 370
Reindeer: 346

Page 9
1) 6, 2) 8, 3) 17, 4) 12, 5) 8, 6) 35p, 7) 40p
Reindeer: 4+9

Page 10
Triangles: a, g, i, m
Quadrilaterals: b, f, h, j
Pentagons: c, k, l, n, p
Hexagons: d, e, o
Reindeer: circle

Page 11
100 + 30 + 4, 200 + 50 + 3, 300 + 20 + 1, 400 + 70 + 2, 500 + 10 + 1, 600 + no tens + 5, 700 + 90 + 1, 800 + 20 + 4, 900 + 80 + 2
Reindeer: one thousand

Page 12
6 x 3 = 18, 4 x 4 = 16, 6 x 1 = 6, 5 x 3 = 15, 6 x 2 = 12, 8 x 3 = 24, 7 x 2 = 14, 9 x 2 = 18, 10 x 5 = 50, 7 x 4 = 28
Reindeer: 3

Page 13
10 ÷ 2 = 5, 20 ÷ 5 = 4, 24 ÷ 3 = 8, 28 ÷ 4 = 7, 45 ÷ 5 = 9, 48 ÷ 4 = 12, 90 ÷ 10 = 9, 27 ÷ 3 = 9
100 ÷10 =10
Reindeer: 3 x 6 = 18, 6 x 3 = 18

Page 14
20, 6, rain, windy, 8, 4;
15, 1,snowballing, 2, 2
Reindeer: snowballing

Page 16
5, 4, 5, 1, 4, 5, 6, 5

Page 17
12.00, 12.10, 12.45, 1.30, 1.50, 2.20, 2.40, 4.00, 4.25, 6.05
Reindeer: 60 mins, 4.45, 4.45, 35 mins

Page 18
16, 24, 9, 15, 6, 8 with 1 left over, 55, 5cm, 2000g
Reindeer: 10 cm

Page 19
10, 25p, 75p £10.00, 35p, £3.40, 7, £5.00
Reindeer: Yes, she has £2.90

Page 20
4000; 300, 20; 3000, 80, 2; 5000, 800, 9; 6000, 40, 1; 7000, 400, 90, 1
Reindeer: Tuesday, Sunday, 1662

Page 21
Reindeer: 9873, 3789

Page 22
>, <, <, >, <, >, <, >
Reindeer: 630, 1603, 1638, 3601, 6803, 16003

Page 23
390, 400, 410, 420, 430; 55, 56, 59, 60, 61; 137, 141, 143, 149; 50, 55, 65, 75, 80; 139, 149, 179, 189; -5, -3, -2, 1
Reindeer: minus 2 each time. or: count back in twos

Page 24
£1.80, £2.95, 73p, £1.32, £6.05, £10.30, £2.20, £1.70
Reindeer: 2705p (£27.05), £12.95

Page 25
Reindeer: £5.00

Page 26
25, 12, 3–4 am; after, 4–5 am, 4–5 am, 118
Reindeer: 236

Page 27
370, 460, 890, 1300, 6320, 7150; 1649; 16490; 13, 25, 97, 160, 555, 719; 15690; 1569
Reindeer: Thirteen; sixteen thousand, four hundred and ninety

Page 28
150g margarine,120g sugar,180g flour, 3 eggs, 60g fruit, 60ml milk
Reindeer: 2.25kg

Page 29
1) cuboid, 2) sphere, 3) pyramid, 4) cube, 5) cylinder, 6) cone; cube; pyramid; cuboid; sphere

Page 31
$\frac{1}{10}, \frac{2}{10}, \frac{1}{4}, \frac{3}{2}, \frac{2}{5}, \frac{3}{3}, \frac{9}{4}, \frac{6}{10}; \frac{3}{8}, \frac{2}{6}, \frac{5}{6}, \frac{2}{10},$
$\frac{2}{8}, \frac{2}{10}$
Reindeer: $\frac{2}{3}$ and $\frac{3}{8}$

Page 32
9.10, 10.30, 11.10, 11.25; Draw clock with hands (see page 64)
Reindeer: £49.28, 72p

Page 33
1) 12, 6p, 2) 305;   3) 5 weeks; 4) $\frac{1}{3}$; 5) 329 + 84= 413; 6) £16; 7) 350, 420, 710, 560, 790; 8) 44, 9) 12; 10) 22nd December
Reindeer: 200 g

Page 34
35,000, 5,000,000, 308,000, 64,400, 3,004,200, 1,300,000, fifty thousand; five million; five thousand; five million, fifty thousand and fifty; five hundred and five thousand and fifty; five hundred thousand and five hundred.
Reindeer: hundreds of thousands; tens of thousands; thousands; hundreds; tens.

© Irene Yates
www.brilliantpublications.co.uk

Answers

Page 35
5, 10, 15, 20, 25, 30, 35, 40, 45, 50;
7, 14, 21, 28, 35, 42, 49, 56, 63, 70;
9, 18, 27, 36, 45, 54, 63, 72, 81, 90;
12, 24, 36, 48, 60, 72, 84, 96, 108, 120
Reindeer: 40, 63

Page 36
1, 2, 3, 4, 6, 8, 12, 16, 24, 48;
1, 2, 4, 8, 16, 32, 64;
1, 9, 5, 3, 15, 45;
1, 9, 3, 27, 81;
1, 2, 3, 4, 6, 9, 18, 12, 36;
1, 5, 25
Reindeer: He will have a remainder or it's a prime number

Page 37
1000 g, 20, 5, 2, 25, 40, 40, 400, 5, 100
Reindeer: 1.75kg

Page 38
$\frac{1}{2}, \frac{3}{4}, \frac{1}{2}, \frac{2}{3}, \frac{1}{2}, \frac{3}{4}, \frac{2}{3}, \frac{3}{4}, \frac{2}{3}, \frac{3}{4}, \frac{1}{2}, \frac{2}{3}$

Reindeer: $\frac{3}{12}$ or $\frac{1}{4}$

Page 39
=, >, >; <, =, =;
$1\frac{2}{5}, 2\frac{7}{10}, 2\frac{1}{4}, 4, \frac{11}{4}, \frac{13}{8}, \frac{5}{3}, \frac{7}{4}$
Reindeer: $1\frac{1}{3}$

Page 40
3; 1) 3, 2) 8, 3) 9, 4) 4 of each
Reindeer: 12

Page 41
2 hours 10 minutes; 150 g, $1\frac{1}{4}$ tbs
7, 4
Reindeer: 48

Page 42
1) 80, 2) Friday, 3) 340, 4) Sunday,
5) 170, 6) 420, 7) 70, 8) 20
Reindeer: £3150.00

Page 43
Friday, Friday, 170, 180, second, 10, 60, Tuesday in week 1.

Page 44
£2.52, £9.98, £7.59, £4.40, £5.95, £2.75, 11, £1.30
Reindeer: £36.58; £9.50

Page 45
Answers down columns
81, 56, 9, 72, 9, 8, 49, 6: 5, 8, 48,
9, 63, 42, 8, 35; 27, 7, 7, 54, 32, 7,
64, 10
Reindeer: 423, 41

Page 46
Joined christmas stars (see page 64)
Reindeer: $2\frac{4}{5}$
because $2.6 = 2\frac{6}{10} = 2\frac{3}{5}$

Page 47
Check shapes

Page 48
1) 58, 2) 210, 3) 4.1, 4) 9,024,
5) 10, 6) 207, 7) 5.2, 8) 8000
9) 90,990, 10) 4100, 11) 99,990
Reindeer: 10, 100, 1000

Page 49
1) 16:29, 2) 08:09, 3) 18:05, 4) 04:26,
5) 11:55, 6) 17:10, 7) 23:53, 8) 21:40,
9) 09:50, 10) 19:10, 11) 06:20,
12) 03:57, 13) 01:15, 14) 07:10,
15) 00:02, 16) 20.15, 17) 02:25,
18) 10:20, 19) 22:20, 05.00
Reindeer: 02:25

Page 50
4, 25, 9, 64, 81, 144, 1, 16, 49, 5,
100, 9^2, 6^2, 121, 36, 8^2, 3^2, 10^2
Reindeer: 144 square cm or 144 cm^2

Page 51
63500, 29800, 11180, 650500, 935,
2170; 56, 236, 10.94, 261, 460,
53.18; 62000, 698000, 9050, 3,
9050, 413000, 2731000; 492,
341.8, 31.5, 1533, 0.074, 0.05
Reindeer: 43.91, 4

Page 52
Missing number puzzles
(See page 64)

Page 53
1) 4.4 metres, 2) £46.69, £3.31,
3) 425.5 km, 4) 7, 5) 15, 6) £1.56
Reindeer: 5 pots

Page 54
3 mince pies, 9 yule logs; 12 trifles,
6 ice creams; 6 green crackers,
8 blue crackers
Reindeer: 20

Page 55
1) $\frac{2}{24}$ or $\frac{1}{12}$; 2) 2, $\frac{1}{3}$; 3) $\frac{2}{5}$; 4) $\frac{1}{10}$;
5) $\frac{6}{30}$ or $\frac{1}{5}$; 6) $\frac{27}{36}$ or $\frac{3}{4}$
Reindeer: shopping $\frac{4}{12}$ or $\frac{1}{3}$;
football $\frac{5}{12}$; nap $\frac{3}{12}$ or $\frac{1}{4}$

Page 56
1) 4384, 2) 1562, 3) 387, 4) 62,
5) 117, 6) 49, 7) 750, 8) 547, 9)
761, 10) 0, 11) 35, 12) 852, 13)
824, 14) 65, 15) 187, 16)138, 17)
825, 18) 660, 19) 299, 20) 9901
Reindeer: 108

Page 57
square, rectangle, rhombus, kite,
parallelogram, trapezium
Reindeer: a square has four right
angles, a rhombus has opposite
angles equal.

Page 58
$\frac{3}{5}; \frac{3}{7}; \frac{1}{3}; \frac{3}{5}; \frac{1}{4}; \frac{1}{4}; \frac{4}{5}; \frac{3}{5}; \frac{2}{3}$
Reindeer: various

Page 59
153290/153300/153000;
987520/987500/988000;
612000/612000/612000;
794690/794700/795000;
1458450/1458500/1458000;
92650/92700/93000;
415470/ 415500/415000;
655460/655500/655000
Reindeer: Twenty three million,
four hundred and sixty seven
thousand

Page 60
1) 3 hrs 15mins, 2) 1 hr 10 mins,
3) 9.40 am, 4) 3.30 pm,
5) 5 hours, 6) 12.05 am
Reindeer: 1 hour, 10 minutes

Page 61
Izzy NE, Assia WSW, Josh NNE,
Dan S, Henry ENE, Sam SSW,
Lisa ESE, Hannah W, Charlotte
E, Tom N, Sophie SSE, Jack
WNW, Mandeep SE, Trish NW,
Chloe NNW, Gemma SW

© Irene Yates
www.brilliantpublications.co.uk

Answers

Page 32
Draw Clock with hands ▼

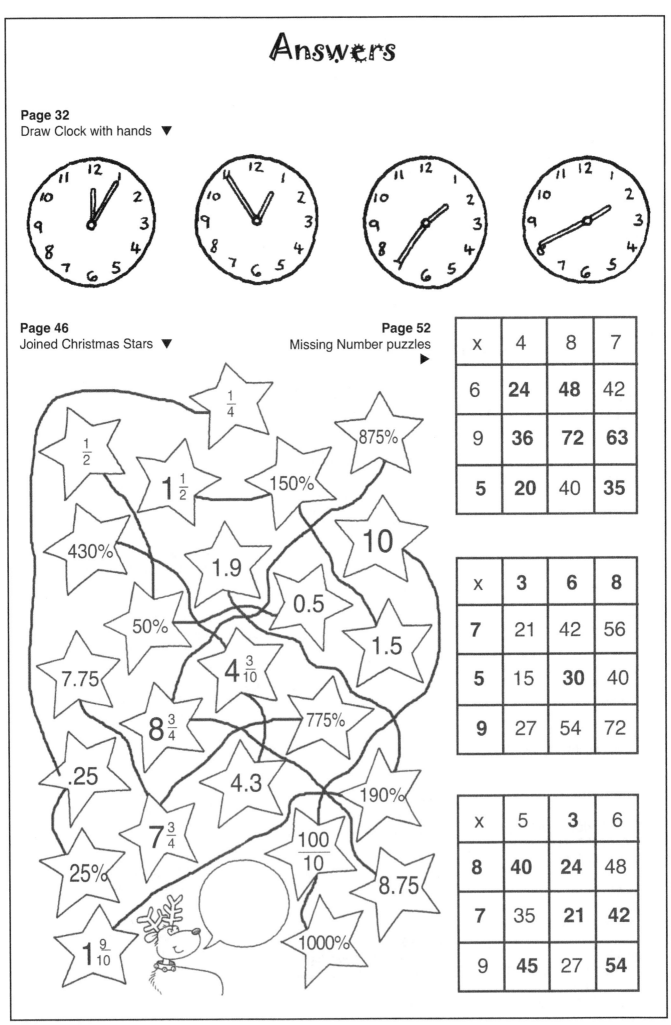

Page 46
Joined Christmas Stars ▼

Page 52
Missing Number puzzles ▶

x	4	8	7
6	**24**	**48**	42
9	**36**	**72**	**63**
5	**20**	40	**35**

x	**3**	**6**	**8**
7	21	42	56
5	15	**30**	40
9	27	54	72

x	5	**3**	6
8	**40**	**24**	48
7	35	**21**	**42**
9	**45**	27	**54**

Stars:
$\frac{1}{2}$ $\frac{1}{4}$ 875% $1\frac{1}{2}$ 150% 430% 1.9 10 50% 0.5 1.5 7.75 $4\frac{3}{10}$ $8\frac{3}{4}$ 775% .25 4.3 190% $7\frac{3}{4}$ $\frac{100}{10}$ 8.75 25% 1000% $1\frac{9}{10}$

Lightning Source UK Ltd.
Milton Keynes UK
UKOW06f0647221113

221597UK00002B/16/P

9 781903 853696